RICHARD HOWARD was born in Cleveland and
was educated at Columbia University and the
Sorbonne. He has travelled widely abroad and lives
now in New York City. His poems and criticism have
been published in many periodicals, including *Poetry,
The New Yorker, Paris Review, The New Republic,*
and *Quarterly Review;* and for a number of years he
was active as a translator of French literature. He was
a Guggenheim Fellow in poetry for 1966–1967, and
is one of the poets published in the first issue of *The
American Literary Anthology,* sponsored by The
National Endowment of the Arts. *Unfinished Poets,*
his study of American poetry since 1950, was
published by Horizon Press. *The Damages,* Mr.
Howard's second volume of poems, was published by
Wesleyan University Press in 1967.

QUANTITIES

Wesleyan University Press

MIDDLETOWN, CONNECTICUT

Quantities

POEMS BY

RICHARD HOWARD

Library of Congress Catalog Card Number: 62–18342
Manufactured in the United States of America
First printing October 1962; second printing May 1968

To Anne and John Hollander

The mind uncertain of its meat
The heart's law in dispute

CONTENTS

QUANTITIES

This leaf, delivered to your empty hand,
Is crumpled like a letter from the fall:
Unfold it gently, it is legible
If you are patient with mortality.
Perhaps it bears a message for your loss

Among its broken veins. Here is a grub
Of summer, modest in its public state
But growing by a private appetite
To prouder life. If property is theft
As Proudhon claimed, the proof is in his jaws—

A larceny of leaves. What grub can own
Grub eats, and eats away the rest to weave
A serviceable shroud against the cold.
The larva, not quite wool, but not yet will,
Is wrapped up well between his other lives.

Would you, like him, survive at any cost?
Then seal yourself in layers of yourself,
Warm as a worm, until there is enough
To eat your heart away and still have left
Enough for the hungriest winter and beyond.

*Jubilary Ode on the Hundredth Anniversary
of the Birth of Marlene Dietrich*

And even after hours
Of waking and a little sleep,
When you by impulse walk
Abroad some natural morning
Or immoderate night,
So fondly will the earth adjust
Its formal longitudes
To fit your stride; so freely will
The light consent to fall
In with your way of looking at
The world; so willingly
Water itself run up to your
Dry mouth (as for dear life)
When you would drink: it is as if
You slept through every one
Of all the ages requisite
To raise the bright trapeze
Of blood within your body, hang
Your acrobatic eyes
From the still unruined arches
That chamber in your skull.

Like love in Shelley, moving with
The easy unconcern
Of its own motion, the purpose
Of your overpowered
Self lives upon itself, and each
Excess of separate
Feature balks some other of its
Singular growth by a
Kind of general song. There is
An innocence in such

Accord, a music I can hear
    Beyond our carnival
And all its obstreperous cries.
    Simple to tell by your
Breathing, by your heart's meters, that
    You are no accomplice
(The record makes it clear—you were
    Erroneously charged)
In our crime of being Somewhere
    The night of Anytime.

Beyond the emblems of your state—
    This corkscrew crossed upon
Its like within a looking glass—
    I see only a blank
Ground without shadows, as one of
    Flat gold: the heraldic
Heaven without a star in it.
    For if there should be stars
What constellation could they cut
    Upon that abstract air—
What zodiacal beast assume
    The rigor of your pose?
Exhibit X in the endless
    Alphabet of our loss,
You find yourself on the unsworn
    But unperjurable
Witness stand of life: not merely
    Overripe or raw, no
Longer hiding out, like us, but
    In your undistracted
Flesh and fabulous bones At Home.

And as I watch you living in
    Your skin like birds that take
The accustomed air of summer
    With no evident need
Or care, it is a cool comfort
    I derive from noting
How for your amusement (always
    At our expense) the best
Seats in the house have been reserved
    For you ahead of Time.

Drastic in its claims upon
Our two-dimensioned holiday
Where sea and sky so neatly hinge,

Your body standing in the sun
Becomes a site of sudden change,
Accuses where we would applaud,

And criticizes every hour
Of light with shadows adequate
To prove the flattened air a fraud.

You walk across the stony beach,
Appropriately negligent
Of effort, and in spite of each

Inhuman task I summon up
To justify men being here,
Facility, I see, is all:

Where one tall bather is enough
To be our season's Centaur, just
By wading slowly out to where

The sea's green fur begins at length
To grow against you, and your own
Accustomed skin gives way to end

In a flourish of salt, swart hair.
How well the unsaddled ocean serves
As stallion half to the human beast!

And for the time we idly stare,
You leave Connecticut behind
With an obsolete shirt and socks and us

On shore—to join the heroes you
Have never heard of in the sea,
Irrelevant as any myth

To all our merely human loves.

Teach us, please, appropriate movements, drill
the hard declensions like a grammar, broken word by word
until at last we grow into the speech
You have granted. Trivial Venus, help us, for we come
unsuited to the custom of our blood
and the other juices. Extenuate our carelessness
especially now, when promise of green
weather rends the lymph: show us a way wholly to mend.
    Mourn
with us for the lost teddy bear; collect
the serpent and the unmentionable duck from our bath,
and restore the doll banished whenever
we cried at parties or would not say Thank You. Intercede
for us: we shall lose our hair. Comfort us
with stomachs: we shall be unhappy. Accord something more
than a useful failure, discover in
us the habit of your moving Law: send us from ourselves.
Possess, Lady, for we are every one
sealed in the envelope You give. O Goddess, intervene!

It was in Karnak. We had ridden out,
Helene and I, after a hurried dinner.
The guide reined in: Avenue of Sphinxes,
Obelisk—oh, I never felt so much

a member of the moon's world! (Can you be growing
in me, Greatness? You were too much for me
Even then!) Is travel—search? Then this was a find.
The watchman at the entrance gave us the first

clue to the startling scale. How silly he looked
beneath the unchecked self-assertiveness
of the gate. And now, to last out our lives,
the pillars—take that one! Wasn't it enough?

Ruin excused what would have been too high
for the highest roof. It stood and held up
Egypt and night. The following fellaheen,
luckily, hung back. We needed time

to put up with this, it was almost a blow
that such a *stance* could still be part
of the being we die in. If I had a son
I'd send him here (when it comes time to learn

things that have to be true for yourself):
"There it is, Charles. Walk past the Pylon,
turn and look . . ."
                              Why doesn't it help *us* more?

That we could bear it at all was something
—a lot—for the two of us, you looking ghostly

in your linen duster, silent, ailing,
and I very much the hermit in my theory.

Still, the mercy of it! Remember the pond
with the obsidian cats sitting around it,
monuments—to What? Presences, then,
and so committed to that magic square

that if five, on one side, hadn't been knocked
over (weren't you flabbergasted too?)
they would have held their Court just as they were—
feline, stony, mute. Everything here

was judgment. Excommunicated pond,
the giant Scarab perched on its rim,
and along the walls the epic boastfulness
of kings: Judgment. And yet at the same time

Reprieve—who would have believed it? As figure
after figure took the clear moonlight,
the carving, every outline accurately
hollowed by shadows to a kind of trough,

became a Vessel, held and yet withheld
what was never witnessed, never hidden:
it, the Secret, so secret in being there was
—needed to be—nothing secretive about it!

The books just leaf past it; no one reads
anything so obvious in a book
(what use is it, looking for a name):
the Unmeasurable forced into the measure

of sacrifice. Just look: what is Possession
until it has learned to give itself away?
Tout passe—things. Help things on their way
and keep your own life from leaking out

some crack or other. Always be the giver.
Herds of asses, humpback bullocks, crowd
to the place where the image—King's, God's—
childlike receives and smiles. His sanctity

is never out of breath. He takes and takes
yet lenity is his law, and often will
the Princess merely clasp the papyrus bloom
instead of snapping the stalk. *Here* all

sacrificial ways abruptly end,
the Sabbath begins, uncomprehended by
the long weeks. Here man and beast
drag off gains the God knows nothing of.

Business is business, and may be,
however high the interest, profitable;
we try and try (the earth can be procured)
but giving only price, give up the prize.

Beds are made close to a wall
   flat
Against the blank places.
This is so that most faces
Can turn away from all
   that.

If I turn, the time swarms.
   Word
Of mouth carries the message
Up and down the soft passage
From a hive that hums
   hard.

I am not lonely here:
   fear
Dissolves in mirrors, some
Dangers melt like sweet salve
On a wound. You must have
   come.

He speaks of a white room showing
Barest at night, shadowed only
By the lamp under which his cat,
White as well, warms in a brightness
Of refusals. Of course there are
Imperfections, but until now
He has been able to shut them
Up or away, into darkness
Behind the blank of his white doors.

Naturally we all suspect
Some other sort of chamber where
He works his living out, warden
Of an implicating space: not
Only purple with unexplained
Obscurities, but gathering
All time in images of dim
Insistences. A various
Room, and full of forms, reflections.

But the truth is down a long hall
And in another place. Here are
Cruel colors, terrible cold
And a burning quite as extreme.
On the changeable bed someone
Else is lying and lying quite
Miserably. Now, following
Trials of temperature, come
Tests on teeth, examination

Nail by broken nail, and nightly
Obligation to employ each
Bright instrument that hangs upon

Its hook. This is a right surround,
Binding blur to brutality—
The genuine decor. How pat
Our word *apartment* falls in here,
For this is the life he divides
From the others, a death apart.

What since August, when the sound
Of bees filled the lindens
And broke like a hot
Berry rotten
In ripeness
Where we
Lay,
What
After
Late motions
Of the sun, what
Grief on the hills, what
Chill stiffening the stream
Changes our love thus to our loss?

We have outgrown the weather;
The months have made only
Diminishing days.
Questioning, we
Were eager,
And grave,
But
Now,
Given
Our wan tact
And the wasting
Of fevers, who could
Hope to print Hell's lavish
Product on a face of snow?

I do not know how we fell,
Having once embellished
Every bud with bloom;
Yet if sap runs
At the root
Of time,
Down
Where
The dark
And warm life
Hides away, then
May we grow again,
Re-according by light
The heart of our green season.

A sense of Fall without the trees
That make their rot so decorous,
A lot of ashes in the air
Tasting oddly of surrender—
This is the place, appropriate
For such unsightly men as these,
Dispossessed and almost holy,
Almost depraved, playing games
Against each other for the long
Chances of a little gain
This afternoon upon the clay.

The river hauls its burdens down,
Lapping greedily like doubt
Between the banks of ashes. Here
They are playing, the mad ruined tribe:
Ignorant, not innocent, and yet
So terribly sure of who they are.
For them it must be difficult
Believing in death, at least before
The sunset, when the opportune light
Hangs like a victim so long in the sky
That all reminders of the dark are dumb.

The old men play until I think
Their laughter is the bravest sport
I ever listened to in nature;
For if their triumph gathers out
Of what is merely argument
To us, the very ground on which
They play is merely graves to them.
Ask of their broken faces, How

Do you savor life? Do you enjoy?
And as one mouth each scar will answer,
Crying, 'I appreciate pain.'

Listen to their voices, words
Echoing over the gritty court:
Something has been given up
But they are playing. While I stand
And watch their game, the western clouds
Accumulate and the world turns back
Into its empty sky, judging
Not as the judge judges, but as
The failing light decides, falling
At last with the exhausted sun
In shadows round a helpless thing.

Wandering with you the shore
That parallels our river
    Like a second thought,
Singular and sad I wore
The habit of a lover
    Almost inside out.

Night in its black behaving
Muffled every lamp and dyed
    The wooly season,
Pig-iron boats were leaving
For the lake, slowly the loud
    Bridges had risen:

A landscape for the lonely
Or the lewd, as you observed,
    When of a sudden
Something steep and with only
Momentary warning moved
    Out of the hidden

Harbor. It was a dark boat
And *Cytherea* it said
    Low on the long bow.
"A cabin for two," cried out
A voice, and I saw a head
    That I thought I knew—

"Fifteen days to the Island:
We sail tonight with the tide!"
    I remember now,
Turning, how your face went blind.

The river sighed in its bed
    And although a few

Gulls were loud in their abuse
You did not once look up. When
    To their obloquy
No protest was made, I chose
To learn what I've always known:
    We shall never go.

Hairy

Here is a roughened instance
    for distrust
Growing upon me, a sense
    of reversed
Intentions, something exposed
    that should lie
Hid, but flourishes ever
    as summer's
Ripest weed. It is an old
    problem, how
To divide the truthfully
    bare from the
Barely true—all surfaces
    are something
Of a paradox, whether
    cumbered like
Mine with this irrelevant
    camouflage
Or naked as your own. Which
    approaches
The honesty of bone? I know
    one answer
Only, for myself. The hair
    that darkens
On my simple skin informs
    the round skull
And my red desiring heart
    with the same
Black fur: this ragged edge and
    lunatic
Fringe are all the body bears
    to show of
A gaining outer darkness.

I   ÉLOGE DE GLAUCE À SCYLLE, NIMPHE DANSANTE

Eyelids flicker to create
Flame upon her cheek.
Phosphors palpitate
As I speak

And the lady is lifted
By a darker dancer;
Quick and explicit, as if in answer,
Ardor has shifted

Flesh, deployed the bone—
So would she discommode
The body to bright stone
Alive: a line, a node

Until before me as I stayed
A salamander careless played
And lay and shrank not from the fire:
'Tis Venus' worm, and represents desire.

II   TU ES SAVANTE, DOULCE ET VERTUEUSE

Gather up the growth of day
Dressed in summer, silk and scent,
         Indolent lady.

Gray and blue veils slide away:
Are you the greenest continent,
         Tropical lady?

Ripe the human colors lay
Where she fell impenitent,
         Declining lady.

III SEULE VOUS SEREZ MA DERNIÈRE AVANTURE

Lounging maples will arrange
Our fall: the greenest hinge

Of summer once undone, there is
A god no longer in the weather's house.

Have we not seen how maples, red
Or leaking gold as if they bled,

Swung on their spindles, slackened,
Spun and fell in cadence likened

To a bright and blurred chorale,
Comic colors at a festival?

IV RESSEMBLANCES DANS UNE GROTTE

How easy, in the cavern, where we lay
Dividing lavish senses into clay

And darkness, to extemporize a world.
The crusted shells, for instance, curled

Around the iridescence of their cause—
Were they not likenesses, a soft applause

Of matter at its own sure imagery
Collected in that cavern where we lay?

Imagine the bivalves there (whose slippery ears
Were seemings of our own), some pink and clear

Or pale as any further flesh of yours,
And others reddened as if from the source

Of cordial rhythms in a qualm of cold:
Such were our semblances, the oyster world

Of lovers in a quiet place; yet one
Sweet mollusc in that clammy cave, upon

Comparison . . .
                        comparisons are dumb.

V LES DEUX AMANTS DESSOUS LE VENT
  D'AUTOMNE

"Chaos of Archaic Change": a garden
And a garden faun, ingloriously streaked
Or else beneath the lindens cracked
By saturated leaves, the burden

Of a dropping season and a gray—
Prophesying, I should say, a bitter
Sequel to the old weeks' weather
And our burning time of day:

Leaves and hours will fail together,
Ruined on the bright pond water.

Water is sour, the air is lonely here
And all the noises of this natural shire
From stable or from sty are not enough:
The ear has memories of its own and will
Not drown. I think you'd better give it up—
Question the local gentry. Go away.

Perhaps I *have* a certain chamber, one
That has no walls. The light is modified
Only by the bodies of my guests
Orderly hung, in solace for their time,
Their fever and their loss. Do not become
Another; it is dark already here.

I was glad when they came at first, every day
Moving among the animals like kin:
We would be happy, and not scared or bored.
But who killed the dogs? Who bribed my bird
With poison? Luckily there is no map
And no one ever finds me any more.

Must they all appear, awkward, to end
In the same defeat? I could not recall
Which was which any more: attitudes
Resemble, all the shadows turn to gray.
What power, what weaknesses provoke
Continuing visits and continuing pain?

I cannot answer, I can only warn.
Who comes to me with a cordial body, spine
And skull and every incidental grace,
Departs by dirty postern gate, slow,

Rumpled and no longer white or red.
You are as lovely as some, as ugly as all,

And will not linger, though absurdly brave,
Longer than the rest have stayed, but grow
Like your artful or barbaric friends
Sick and tired. Let no special sting
Offend you; it is not a personal death
At my hands you suffer, nor a private life.

Wilderness precedes
    Any wisdom
Worth the name: our needs
    Are not the same

For a graveyard as
    In the forest,
But until we pass
    Among the most

Scandalous leaves, what
    Good are all these
Quaint beds, clipped and not
    Climbing? Unless

Any wasted place
    To start with is
As foul on the face
    Of it as this,

I came from the worst;
    Having entered
The tangle and got lost,
    I encountered

The local serpent
    Followed by apes,
Bears, and the red ant
    That nothing stops,

Unopposable
    In fierceness. Such
Denizens were all
    Expected, each

To be met with in
   Anybody's
Jungle. But sudden
   And unlike these

Looked-for claws and howl
   Were you, the last
I came upon, well
   Met and the first

To offer comfort:
   No less creature
For all that, a part
   Still of the bare

Trees and the twisted
   Region I live
Within—yet I would
   Swear the wood dove

Sang out, the light gained
   At our meeting,
And then all the land
   Turned from its long

Wars with the darkness
   To a clearing.
Perhaps now it is
   Still a raw thing

To claim as my own
   The orderly
Growth about me, when
   I had met the

Bright heraldic beast
In another
Part of the forest
Altogether,

But observing now
The developed
Roots of days, and how
The sun has tipped

Each conforming tree
With autumn, is
It not wise to see
In wilderness

The enacted course
Of our burdens
And the greenest source
Of all gardens?

To compose the reality of shadow
 Requires a light;
Even the ashes of exhausted evenings,
 Wearing the weight
And consequence of ice, glow again for some
 Kinds of coal. What
Fed the fire among such bare and broken trees
 I saw one night?
It was perhaps a dream growing in darkness
 Like the red flight
Of summer after spring: you had walked within
 The flare of bright
Torches, and the glassy particles of love
 Melted in the heat
Of every line. After you the fire died down,
 The cold was very great.

It is the movement that disturbs the line,
    Thickening the form,
    Turning into warm
Compression what had once been cold and fine.

Seen from down here, if only we remained,
    These hills are high:
    Driving on, the sky
Imposes and no longer can be trained

By any structure of the seeming ground.
    Landscape, I discover,
    As the car gains over
Something that changes from a little mound

To monstrous eminence before your eyes,
    Landscape can flaunt, can
    Foil like a courtisan:
And when you see the difference in size

Of cliffs we once considered at the bright
    Grass along their peak
    And then saw from the bleak
Extremity of sand below, the sight

Gives more than pause—alas, it gives the slow
    Ruin of our hopes
    Fed upon the slopes
From where we've been to where we want to go.

No matter how
Numb or practiced,
Even the most
Skillful mouths are
Merely the scars
Of love, wholly
Obedient
To the bending
Heart, hardly more
Than wounds outworn.
In the landscape
Of your crowded
Head, for instance,
Every feature
Will conform close
To a future
Weather, carving
Geologies
Of pain just where
The surprising
Lakes, monadnocks
And long ravines
Decisively
Appear, starting
Forth together
Here, to finish
Elsewhere as if
Sorted into
Separate rocks,
Clean forgotten
And far away;
There, for all we
Know of its fine

Terminations,
Our buried and
Familiar blood
Lies in a cold
Tangle—apart,
Dry, dumb. Seeing
At this distance
How flesh and bone
Must grow into
Division, chilled
Beneath the weight
Of sudden snow
And lost to their
Intended laws—
Seeing so near
The coming wreck,
I think of that
Ground we rot in
All, and stare at
The giving soil:
Faults in strata
Show like success,
Life is very
Terrible, as
Our faces know.

Music is one means of telling time
    That forces memory
To conjugate the tenses of the mind
    In terms of moving sound:
When I hear music, all I was I am.

Love, I think, has something of the same
    Effect, the other way
Around, permitting what has not yet been
    To come into its own:
With you, my love, what I will be I am.

Decay is in the poplar,
    Darkness gathers
On even the simplest
    Leaf, and withers.

Never in this climate
    Of loss before
Could I have ascended
    To where you are

Standing—a place beyond
    Our foul weather
And all freezing. Yet I
    Have another

Comfort still to take, more
    Than keeping well
Or merely warm: ever
    Curious of all

Determinations, how
    Must I name this
Time and know this season?
    Like travellers

And other such strangers,
   Calling places
They came to by titles
   Of the countries

They had lost, can I do
   Else in the wrong
Weather but look up and
   Label it spring?

De Manus Fabrica

for Andreas Vesalius

Where the knuckles rise like Apennines
From an umber undersod,
Where the blood so abruptly loosens
All its lakes about these sudden bones,
Apprentice, mark your lesson
With the signature of life: beneath
A circumstantial skin, cut
To the shrinking center of this hand.

This hand . . . It is a body without politics,
A no man's land for the queer
Companionable creatures that swarm
In silent flocks through every fervent cell—
Freaks of talent, erratic
Virtuosi of the lymph, forcing
The merest flesh to fortune
And the mightiest to its flaw.

Only the bone is orthodox, submits
To condemnations of the will:
White Isolde renounces and dies
Rigid in her joy as any warp
Of wave-whitened rib, a bone
No longer contended for by bones.
And when Saint Catherine hung
In splinters on her wheel, the blood

Draining off like memory, then at last
She found the dry detachment
Of pure desire. Now, apprentice,

Take a living hand; learn from it how
Upon love's skeleton, within
The protocol of bones unwavering
And white, some red imperfect
Self must keep us wet and keep us warm.

What wind there was this morning
And what rain
Betrayed the bitter month they met in—
Of course there was no sun.

The darkness spared no symptom
Of its pain,
No parturition. Whatever birth
Might trouble the black earth

Was not to be witnessed beyond
My own brain;
The flesh was out of question, frozen hard.
Alone, the mind had heard

Suggestive noises: two days
Only, but
Two marked by abandoned cold, have passed
Clattering since I last

Was with you. For those two days
I have not
Laid an eye, a hand, a mouth upon
You, and stare at the wan

Prospect of as many days
Done without
You as there will be days at all. Now,
Ruined by rain, I know

How neglect in our season
Of absence
Changes to weight of terrible frost,
And I guess how the first

Or even the ultimate
Evidence
Of loss grows light in charitable
Weather: then will the free

Enterprise of a green earth
Draw my sense
Down to a common fall, overthrown
While the sun looks on, cooks on.

Of the four elements
    only fire destroys,
Proving what we warm to
    in the winter as
A reassuring sign
    of life and increase
Is merely the bright rack
    and ruin of our
Broken world. I would take
    another emblem—
Say salt, to awaken
    the various grace
And flavor of the field
    I walk in now. But
No sowing, even to blind
    depths in the furrow,
Can bring one sprout from salt.
    Though my rough weeds grow
Into savor by its
    mediation, which
Can flourish long in such
    blank epitome?
Where is a source, a well?
    What rain I cry for
Cools the rancid weather?
    Even though you give
Water to drown my salt,
    dissolve such embers,
Still am I white in my
    mineral burning,

Or in cinder blackened:
    these ashes prevail.
Turn my tables today
    and the root I eat
Is bitter; burn down my
    house tomorrow, what
Will I carry away?
    I would save the fire.

I HOSTESS' SONG

Waking wild-eyed in the morning
    I remember how we met,
How the records needed turning
    And the oven wouldn't shut.
Everyone enjoyed the party
    Though: they stayed till after three
(It was hellish in the city
    And my drinks were strong. And free).

When the neighbors phoned at midnight
    To complain about the noise,
I replied (so grandly!) "Drop it
    In the mailbox with the keys."
Half the cigarettes were drowned when
    Helen spilled the best champagne:
Damned if Larry's ever going to
    Make me ask that girl again!

All the tables need restaining
    Where the parakeet was "sick";
Someone left the water running
    And the kitchen is a wreck!
Two umbrellas in the closet
    Never were (or will be) mine.
I must make a little visit
    To my bank right after ten.

Meanwhile, reckoning a shambles
    That is worthy of Pompeii,
Where the melted ice resembles
    All that's left of Lidice,

I recall the ancient order
    Which presided when you came—
How you happily regarded
    The appointments of my home.

Now you're lying in the bedroom
    And your face is rather gray,
Its expression—what an emblem
    Of the dreams of yesterday!
I apologize for dinner
    (Only two or three were ill)
—You will find the bromoquinine
    In the bathroom down the hall.

The Penates have disowned us,
    And some other gods as well
Have explicitly abandoned
    What remains of mortal will.
Undisguised by easy living
    In the difficult light of dawn,
"Man's Estate" in there is having
    Trouble staying in his skin.

If the Powers that plumped our pillow
    And contrived this bedding-down
Gave a thought to what must follow,
    How amused they might have been:
Once the sacred passions climax
    And the proud *afflatus* goes,
How unwieldy these poor relics—
    Purely human mysteries.

54

II QUEER'S SONG

Floating, face up, on the open
    Estuary
Of sleep, you wait for it to happen.
    You are very

Beautiful, stupid, and alone
    Now at the source
Of all the loneliness we learn
    From someone else.

For you the darkness does its part—
    Arms fall, and eyes,
And the heart proves by its lack an art
    The mouth supplies.

Sleep then, or feign to, as you drown
    And I pursue
Your blood to its filthy cellar down
    In the hollow

Hairy places. Here shall I feed
    Where every sense,
Handmaid and Hangman to your need,
    Is audience.

III MUSICIAN'S SONG

Some we know play trumpets
    In a public place;
Some to please extend their knees
    Around a double bass.

Some discover concord
　　In a perfect fourth;
Some from cellos, some from bellows
　　Make their money's worth.
Some I've heard played loudly
　　(They were not the best);
One or two—none sweet as you—
　　Played sweeter than the rest.

Cautious critics tell us
　　In the pieces prized
Virtuosos never rose so
　　High as advertised;
Better choose a program
　　Something less than pro—
Connoisseurs, like amateurs,
　　Listen while they blow.

IV　DUET FOR THREE VOICES

Primo:　O whom are you fooling
　　　　　Said Failure to Phony
　　　　What role do you covet
　　　　　You never could play?

Secundo:　I ride on a carrousel
　　　　　Carrying many:
　　　　I want what the others
　　　　　Have given away.

Primo:　And how are you feeling
　　　　　Said Feral to Failure
　　　　What acts have you witnessed
　　　　　What work have you done?

Secundo: Sometimes I regret as I
    Sulk in my cellar
  How much, as I watch them,
    I hate every one.

Primo: Whose cup are you filling
    Said Phony to Feral
  What kind of a doorknob
    Can turn you, my man?

Secundo: In bed where my practice
    Is openly plural
  I seldom leave early—
    Do come if you can.

Una Voce: The night that is falling
    Confirms our disguises
  Determines our calling
    And darkens our grief.

For Failure what future
  For Phony what prizes
For Feral what creature
  Can sanction our life?

V BAWD'S SONG

Our talk in bars is inexact
  Slurring the heart's
    Verb in respect

To voice or person, and exhorts
A tropic motion
In the parts

Needing most refrigeration.
Orderly kinds
Of passion

Come elsewhere—upon our minds
Of course, come
Like old wounds

Covering up their bloody time.
But now and here
Is a scheme

And a scandalous semaphor
Improvable
By no mere

Elocutionary skill:
What diction so
Final and full

As a mouth unfastening into
One such perfect
Empty O?

VI   BLUES

Leaving late I lock up lit
Stammering slightly
Quite unsightly

And half seas over—profligate:
I'm so far out
Of limits that I lately
Relinquish my footing completely,
And this almost nightly.

Time that once consoled us both
For all our bother
Now, I gather,
Devises gin and dry vermouth
(In Wine is Truth)
To jostle us together,
Just one damned thing after another
In a changing weather.

Often reft when left behind
The mind will wander
Wide and slander
Even its own. If mine is found
Floating around
In your flat beer or under
The bar, after taking a gander,
Please Return to Sender.

VII ISLAND BLUES

Lost my love
on one of
the Thousand Islands
(wherever
a river
goes there are islands).
If you are

together
   each of the islands
makes a kind
of mainland.
   Otherwise islands
divide and
conquer. Find
   my love: no islands
for me. Lost
my love last
   night on the islands—
   the Thousand Islands.

It is a bare and crooked
    Tree to heaven
        Growing,
Lovelier perhaps for showing
    Black; but naked
        Even
      So to hold
Such narrow helping from the cold.

I walk round it when I can
    (Barely so smooth,
        So straight
Myself), comforted to equate
    The life of man
        Thus with
      Another's—
Even one that rots or withers.

The branches tremble; living,
    It is never
        The less
A tree such as I could possess,
    A law giving
        Over:
      Not to be,
But becoming; less safe—more free.

In the white season I found
    Proud ornaments
        Pasted
On it. But look how these rusted

Metal pears grind
    Poor dents
In the bark,
Bending the raw twigs fork from fork!

Someone passes—who is it
    Comes now, noble
        Creature:
Is it the King of Spain's daughter
    Come to visit
        Me, all
For the sake
Of my one black tree? Take it back

To Spain! Flourish among almonds,
    My ill-hung tree;
        Impart
To her a less ironic fruit
    Than what you once
        Bore me.
I shall wreathe
Another tree now (barely smooth

Or straight myself) with gold pears
    That cannot waste;
        They grow
Only mortal ones in Spain. How
    Many these tears,
        And lost
    All to win
A tree? Better leave off. No. Begin!

See how the brown kelp withers in air
    Gasping to its death
Upon the salty ice. A moment
    Only was enough
To banish the loveliness that made
    Of a few rather
Inexpressive weeds under water
    A lover's emblem
Of success—easy-moving, soft and
    In the heart's color.

Can simple air become so foul? Now
    After a short time
Parted from warm company we kept
    Together, I share
That condition, a gradual rot
    So far from the sea:
Absence of the proper element
    Will take effect, take
Soon the mouth out of my very words.

Motto on a garden clock
Referring to the twelve hours:
OMNES VULNERANT, NECAT

ULTIMA. Stand close to me
While the sun lasts. By losses
Sustained we come to this grief,

Learning here in a shadow
How we figured—how we shall
Erase. But the last one kills,

The remembered: ULTIMA
NECAT, the sun is going
Down, the faces dim, the dark . . .

Weakness you called it
To cherish this cairn
Of exhausted rocks
I live on, plucking
Quartz from quartz for earth.
Already you left
Your own such mountain,
Had passed along down
The steep eminence
Of old affections,
To discover, sole,
A private landscape
In the plains below.
That is one country
I have never seen,
But can imagine
How you struck terror
And delight upon
The inhabitants,
Casting your shadow
Like a persistent
Obelisk laid low
And long as the sun
Would lengthen it. If
The sun moved, why then
The shadow moved too,
And you never had
Twice the same bed to
Lie in, rest being
Ruin, boredom, fear.
But something stopped you

Once, here you are: can
Weakness hold you now?
I wonder. Though I
Have seldom foraged
From these stones, I grow
Fresh in abiding shade,
And from blue places
Underneath, who knows
What surprising growth
To greet, provided
Shadows stay on me—
Whether broken or whole
I care not, but stay.

Accommodating love with "something still
    Of the sea," he only meant
    To decorate a failure spent
Upon Corinna's bed, from which he went
Away too suddenly to serve it well.

Yet with her for an hour the Cavalier
    Discovered comfort from the cold,
    And found it politic to hold
A warming world against him, though he told
Corinna's maid to call him well before

The King would ride, and time itself return.
    The lovers closeted apace
    And fell together—an embrace
That gathered each unbidden sense to grace,
Though not the kind Corinna's fan could learn.

Thereat the summons of a little bell
    Inconsiderately spread
    Silver tumult overhead.
Corinna laughed, and tidied up her bed;
The laureate subsided with the swell.

In truth love had a semblance of the sea,
    Showing less among the fair
    Ripples of Corinna's hair
Than sharing in the ignorant and bare
Condition of its wreck: a breaking free.

Corinna stirred. She was alone, so closed
 Her cabinet. Perhaps she thought
 How Venus' beauty had been wrought
To birth upon the ocean, later caught
With Mars in Vulcan's net. Corinna dozed.

That night, at Margate, the low water ran
 White on every knocking stone,
 Embittered almost, as if one
God more were gone. It was the very tone
And timbre—somewhat louder—of a man.

Having for some time heard
Nightly in low places
Of incomparable
Creatures that had been hung
Imaginatively
On my heart, disguising
There the boring body
Of a poor impostor,
Having attended to
Whatever bad rumors
Ran among your hopes as
In your most hopeless fears,
You must have expected
The hooded Basilisk
Itself, or the Hydra
Whose rubbery heads are
Likely to penetrate
Anywhere, and supposed
At least the Chimaera
(Which is known for its frauds)
To be among the stale
Myths of a monstrous me.

And this was a mistake.
Later, when you were so
Warmly obliged to give
Away your old fancies,
Was it not difficult
To face the hard choices,
Hating as you did to
Abandon the legend,
The crumbled fairy tales,

In favor of one fact—
The raw rough animal?

Where and to what purpose
Was the story then? Where,
Finding yourself at last
Here, down, and darkened by
A furious human
Creature in a foreign
Skin—where was the bright news,
The chronicle of day?

On the sighing bed, boy,
Something changes the past.
Fictions, even yours, turn
Over and expose. You
Became the myth I was
The moment that I came;
More collapsed with the warm
Deceit than is to be
Recovered: Glaucon or
Antinous—someone
Other!
     And terrible
That I, no magic left
Now, by daylight, discover
You, dead, anonymous
After the night, and cold
In your flesh against me . . .

Manners of this time this place
    moderate me.
Weather grows accustomed, space
    more or less free
To take whatever shape you left
    in the soft air,
Memories of the eyeball fixed
    but not forced there.

It is an anyhow world
    I wander, run
Now to such days, corroding, cold
    for the season
But never too white for spring.

"Staring at the east
Behind the windows of our train,
What is it you see at nightfall?"

"I can see something . . .
It is the falling sun, wrongly
Reflected on this pale heaven,

A red suicide
Descending where, before, the hopes
Of every day mounted to their

Customary wreck.
Looking out with you through the clear
Deception of a moving train,

I see the sunset
Spread upon the east that should be
Blue as any water, just as

With another eye
I see, in the brilliant glass,
Love, like another sun, rising
In the western sky."

I found the same shell, with a frayed root
Grown to strange distortion gripping it,
That I had kicked farther down the beach
Last August. Now, a winter afterward,
Could I, a proper student of the sand,
    Distinguish what was quick
      From corruption?

The valves had not yet quite relinquished
Their hold, adhered still, though only air
Filled their wrecked ovals, and the vise
Of whitened roots that clasped them close
Had suffered from the salt as surely
    As this shell was empty:
      Death hugging death

For dear life, while maybe four feet off
The waves indulged that same display
Of orderly dishevelment I could not fit
My senses to, the skin of dirty lace
Dissolving in a deeper glow of green.
    It was the root-bound shell,
      Mortality,

I remembered while the living water ran
Out of mind, and I forgot the sea.
What will summer be besides a grave
Unless everything we forget, even life,
Makes what we are, just as much
    As anything, even death,
      We remember?

For a Book of Hours

I   AN APRIL AT THE CHÂTEAU DOURDAN

The lady's hand holding a buttercup
Confesses by its bloom against its bud
The beauty of relations still unripe.

Listen, gentles, before the clouds parade
Their music, here's a sharper music come;
A will worth something more than all your game
Of indigo gowns and feathers in the sun
Freshens the espaliers and commends
To ivy the old walls they grow upon—
Something more than a lilac lover
Bends her hand, her garment, and that bright trefoil:

It is the Garden, lady. This is where
Beneath the arches and the spangled air
You fell before the simple earth was full.

II   POL DE LIMBOURG RIDES TO AVIGNON IN MAY

Even the grass bore blossoms and the sun
Rang like a sound of music in the mind,
That day we crossed the woods to Avignon.
Upon the journey, gay and green, we chose
Appropriate amours, and when the wind
Flattered the pale ascent of sycamores
In like ascensions sighing, we discerned
Our journey's lesson in its broken phrase.

Here is a world of bright venereals,
Eager in dominion, opulent
But muted too, whose compromising wills

Accord the count his countess and shall prove
Their match beyond all fops of temperament:

Love is the color of a lady's sleeve.

III   TO JEAN BOURDICHON AT THE OCTOBER SOWING

Beyond those intricate mountains, well beyond
The river in the barley fields where men
And orderly oxen are, the Scorpion

Reaches for a charred and bitter ground
To poison, some unyielding interval
When swans no longer double in the pond
And Anjou is a not quite physical land;

As if the claw of some white principle
Had torn away the unnecessary gold
And with it all our grandiose moving green.

Say then that the zodiac runs on
And that there are not leaves enough to hold—
No matter, Jean, that the ambitious fields grow cold:
The fat is in the fire, the summer sown!

Hurrying the tired heart
From worry tonight homeward
And fast over hills beyond
Here to somewhere eagerly
Else, love, run, run to your rest.

Standing stock-still I marvel
How much you so resemble
The imp of promises I
At best improvidently
Took you for in old weather . . .

Comes the broken time, labels
Even of a light travel
Lie as of a dark. Look how
The burning countries oh far
Away grow black down again.

Change in our weather
Wakened me, the winter struck a chord
Upon its crooked instrument, an owl
Diminished: nothing dared to move.
My clock suggested but it did not tell,
And if there was no witness who could prove
There was a crime? Look how an angry bird
Blackened my bed this morning with the smell
Of burning feathers!

Not the famous fowl
But a lesser phoenix that has left
These ashes in my sheets; I burn him up
To find the creature fire and fear again—
Fire in his hair, fear in his absent cup,
Rara avis! I wonder if the pain
Of April warming on his wings will sift
Such dirty cinders; or will they all drop
Down to make fools

Of the sleepy five
That were my senseless senses. Senses fail;
Observe the hinting clock, the hollow sound
Of music in the dark, then sympathize
With all the birds that celebrate the end
For which they first were made: whatever size
Our incandescent rooster, he must fill
The cavity of sorrow to commend
The whole of love.

If you have received well
you are what you have received.

Ohio from a train
Looked always other; half his way across
The unimportant chain
Of Alleghenies that intended east,
An early morning rain
Made dubious the sky and in its stead,
As if all hope were gone
Of reckoning climate by his calendar,
Ran April like a stain
Across the glass—unfinished, unfulfilled
And frankly alien.

As in the past, today
Landscape and weather were his enemies;
It seemed unlikely they
Would yield. But if in answer to their terms
Of terror he could say
For sure how mountains fell from monstrous size
To minor lumps of clay
Behind his eyes, how every season turned
Within his heart to gray:
This once, perhaps, the darkness too would fall
In less pronounced a way.

He thought how many times
He had construed the weather like a verb,
Declined the rain, that comes
As water will—unasked, but a forgiven guest—
And even in his dreams
Had pressed a grammar on the land. Somehow

They were important themes,
Such wet beginnings as he knew, this earth
That April never seems
To satisfy, the sullen passage of
His unprotesting homes.

Distance made the weather
Disappear. The clouds that filled the sky
Conformed until they were
Illustrious with being. Time was before
Him, no need to hurry
Understanding. Where the towns had loomed
Dark with incoherence
Of houses, the primary colors, after rain,
Startled him to praise. Here
The land grew lovely in the stillness of
Accumulated air,

As one would have it first,
Not later hope occasionally; here
The sun, that had abused
His eyes a moment by the distances
Of moving mountains, placed
Perspectively the shoulders of the earth,
Discovered as he passed
The consequentialities of weed
And water moving west
Against his progress, while his purpose grew
Within him like an East.

Such travelling was true
In parallel. Along the simple tracks
Which accurately flew

Beneath, he followed himself away, away
    From weather came into
That unconditional country of his blood
    Where even landscape grew
Dim as he had never dared to hope,
    And when he breathed he knew
The air as sick men breathe and know the spring:
    Cold still, but coming to.

    Now, the train running on,
He clambered up the enterprising bones
    His body reached him down
So carefully for the ascent, he climbed
    The scaffold skeleton
Up shoulders to the summit of his skull
    (Past marshes overgrown
And hollows filled by sudden rubbishes)
    Until he stared upon
The shore of all his history, as it
    Would look when it was done.

    The clumsy body, where
He had before been always caught, imposed
    An image of its care
Upon the country's custom, made him feel
    (Generous in passing for
Pausing in passing): *only when you leave*
    Will you know where you are.
He travelled, putting distance into sense.
    The mountains fell, and far
Ahead he thought he saw the sea. What if
    It was, if it was there?

Then that was where, tonight,
He wanted to arrive. Thus he would leave
    The suburbs of his heart,
Would come to the capital city where it was.
    The sun became as bright
Above him as the sight could bear. He knew
    It then, that he would find
The fabulous city and the fact of seas
    Already in his mind,
And only there: the landscape lived in him
    As he might live in it.